I0814888

Writing About the Amish

WRITING ABOUT THE AMISH

BETH WISEMAN

THORNDIKE PRESS
A part of Gale, a Cengage Company

To protect the privacy of the Amish folks who helped me with research — some allowing me to take pictures — names and places have been changed to protect their privacy.

Every effort has been made by the author to ensure that the information contained in this book was correct as of press time. The author and publisher hereby disclaim and do not assume liability for any loss, damage, or disruption caused by errors or omissions, regardless of whether any errors or omissions results from negligence, accident, or any other cause. Readers are encouraged to verify any information contained in this book prior to taking any action on the information.

Thorndike Press® Large Print.
The text of this Large Print edition is unabridged.
Other aspects of the book may vary from the original edition.
Set in 19 pt. Plantin.

**LIBRARY OF CONGRESS CIP DATA ON FILE.
CATALOGUING IN PUBLICATION FOR THIS BOOK
IS AVAILABLE FROM THE LIBRARY OF CONGRESS.**

ISBN-13: 978-1-4205-2066-8 (hardcover alk. paper)

Published in 2025 by arrangement with Beth Wiseman.

Print Number: 1 Print Year: 2025
Printed in Mexico

This book is dedicated to all the Amish families who have shared their homes, information, and meals with me. I will be forever grateful for their willingness to assist me in writing stories that glorify God.

FROM THE AUTHOR

How could I have known that my first book — *Plain Perfect* — would set in motion a life-changing sequence of events that would forever change me as a person and alter my life in a way I never could have predicted? What started as a three-book series set in Lancaster County, Pennsylvania, morphed into a career that has spanned over a decade, so far. With over forty published stories, mostly novels and novellas centering around the

Amish way of life, I have learned a lot from the Plain people. From that effort, I've tried to represent the Amish folks as accurately as possible, hoping to mentor to others about God's love and grace, without being preachy or over-the-top. My biggest surprise is, while writing the books, I've unknowingly been ministering to myself. I've gotten to know myself better through a stronger relationship with God, faced fears, acknowledged faults, and accepted God's grace and friendship into my life in a more personal way.

I set out to write one book that might possibly change one life. I've received countless emails and letters suggesting that I have played a part in bettering another person's life and relationship with God. I'm wise enough to know this would be impossible without my Lord and Savior involved in every step of the process.

I have been abundantly blessed, and I try to never take that for granted. As I continue to write stories that I hope will inspire and entertain, I thank my readers for walking alongside me on this amazing journey. Above all else, I thank God for continuing to guide my hand and fill my head with stories that I hope will always glorify Him.

Throughout my journey among the Amish, I have been educated, entertained, and humbled. I've witnessed events that have dropped me to my knees in thanks and prayer. I have also found myself in situations that were humorous and surprising. I hope that you will enjoy traveling with me as I recall some of my favorite happenings with the Amish over the years.

May God's peace and blessings be present in all that you do and all that you are.

~ Beth Wiseman

Are You Amish?

Over the years, I've been asked quite a few times if I am Amish, despite the fact that I'm never wearing traditional Amish clothing. It seems to me that folks fall into one of three categories when it comes to the Plain people. They either know everything there is to know (or claim to), they are still studying and learning (like me), or they don't know anything at all about what it means to be Amish. I didn't know very much about the

Amish, either, when I began writing books about these people who choose to live so differently than us.

Let's start with clothing. It's not universal when it comes to traditional Amish garb. Similar, yes, but not identical. The rules vary from state-to-state and even from district-to-district. Buttons on men's shirts might be allowed in one Amish community, but down the road in another district, it's a no-no. The same things apply to the style of clothing, distinguishing features of the prayer covering — *kapp* as they call it — length of dresses, whether or not dresses are pinned or not, colors allowed, etc.

Here are a few things I've been

called out on over the years. Sometimes the reader was correct, and sometimes I was the one to politely set the inquirer straight.

- Reader: Your cover for *Plain Pursuit* is completely wrong. The boy has buttons on his shirt.
- Me: Panic. I was almost positive buttons were allowed. Sure enough, after researching and talking with a woman who used to be Amish, buttons are allowed in Paradise, Pennsylvania IN THAT DISTRICT. Further down the road, buttons not allowed.
- Reader: That woman's hair on the cover is parted on the side.

All Amish women part their hair in the middle.

- Me: Again, I went back to my friend to ensure that parting a woman's hair on the side is allowed. It is.
- Reader: Your cover model has sculpted eyebrows.
- Me: Oops. The reader was correct. This was a book early in my career. You can probably identify which novel without me telling you.

And, last but not least. A BIG OOPS — My publisher blew up the cover of *Plain Pursuit* (book #2 in the Daughters of the Promise series) to use in an advertising campaign. Imagine my horror when

I saw a wedding ring on the woman's third finger of her left hand. Amish folks do not wear wedding rings or jewelry of any kind. We didn't notice it until the cover was blown up, so the ring was removed, and in all future editions there is no wedding ring. If you own *Plain Pursuit,* look closely at the woman in the background. If you see a wedding ring on her finger, then you have a first edition copy of the book.

So, what would I look like if I were Amish? Turn the page to see for yourself.

Plain Paradise
BETH
WISEMAN
BEST-SELLING AUTHOR OF PLAIN PERFECT

Public Affection

Readers of Amish fiction know that public affection is frowned upon. As an author in this genre, I know the Plain people are modest and don't openly display physical endearment. Well, I guess I forgot.

A friend and I traveled to Lancaster County to do research. We met with several Amish families, and we dined in an Amish home that had housed five generations. The owner was happy to have us stay after the meal to answer questions. She was a lovely woman, very helpful, warm and congenial. We're from Texas, so hugging her when we left that evening felt as natural as breathing. Texans hug everyone. It wasn't awkward at all, and she returned the embrace.

On the day we were scheduled to return home, my friend and I wanted to tell this sweet Amish woman goodbye. We attended an event where we knew she would be. I honestly can't remember the venue. That was over a decade ago, and I've slept since then. But, two things stick out in my mind. First, we were the only non-Amish people there. We found our Amish friend standing outside a building surrounded by a group of other Amish women. Excited, we rushed toward her, excusing ourselves for interrupting, but happy to have found her among the crowd.

After thanking her profusely for spending time with us, I threw my arms around her. I thought I felt her arms tense at her sides, but before I had time to process her reaction, I'd stepped aside. My bubbly friend was next, wrapping the woman in a big bear hug. It was then that I noticed the expressions of the women in the group, their surprised gazes ping-ponging from one to the other. And the woman we hugged turned three shades of red.

I'm not going to say that all of the Plain people resist hugging in public. But I saw and felt a level of unease firsthand, so now I don't hug my Amish friends and acquaintances, privately or otherwise. My intent is to always respect their ways, and I don't want to cross any lines. Perhaps I should have known better. I'd heard about their resistance to any type of public affection. But, I suppose, I was thinking more about romantic kisses, and things like that. Thank goodness I didn't kiss her on the cheek too.

The Town of Intercourse

You can't visit Lancaster County, Pennsylvania, without wandering into the town of Intercourse. This community in the heart of Amish Country was founded in 1754, but it was originally named Cross Keys, which was the name of a local tavern. There are various theories about why the town was renamed in 1814, but perhaps those are to be debated in another book.

When I wrote my first Amish book, *Plain Perfect,* my editor asked me if we could remove the town of Intercourse, citing that it was a distraction while reading the manuscript. At the time, there were only a few authors writing Amish fiction, and the genre was growing, but it hadn't risen to the popularity it is now. I explained to my editor that the town of Intercourse was as popular as the towns of Bird-In-Hand and Paradise, to omit it would be an omission of authenticity to the area. She ultimately allowed the use of Intercourse.

While dining with an Amish family over ten years ago, I wrongly assumed that everyone knew that the word 'intercourse' wasn't just the name of a town. Following a lovely meal, I fell into a casual conversation with an Amish teenage girl. She was interested in my books. I explained to her how my editor had originally wanted me to omit the town of Intercourse from *Plain Perfect.*

"Why would she want you to do that? Intercourse is very popular with the tourists," she told me.

I started to explain to her about the meaning of the word, but when her eyes widened and I felt her mother's eyes on me, I backtracked in a big way. It became obvious that this innocent teenager did not know where I was headed with my explanation so I finagled my way out of an embarrassing moment for everyone.

Now, that might seem far-fetched, but I have another story that supports the naivety of the young people in Amish communities. I was told by a reliable source that a young couple visited their doctor, concerned because the wife had not yet become pregnant. They explained how they had been sleeping together for months without being able to conceive a child. After further evaluation, the doctor learned that the couple had been doing exactly what they said — *sleeping* together — as in closing your eyes and catching some shut-eye. True story. You're probably thinking about how these young people grew up on a farm and were surely educated as to how the reproduction process works. Apparently not.

Pictured (left to right) are Beth, editor Natalie Hanemann, and bestselling author Kelly Long.

An Amish restroom to Remember

I've been in a lot of Amish homes, shops, and bakeries. But one trip to the ladies room in an Amish bakery tops my list.

A friend took me to a bakery where they still use wood ovens for baking. As always, these Plain people were courteous, and the food was amazing. It was definitely an off-the-beaten-path place out in the middle of nowhere. A family member went there often, and she took me along on one of my trips to Indiana. I bought the best fried pies I've ever tasted. I even based my story — *Loaves of Love,* from *An Amish Christmas Bakery* collection — on this very unique bakery. They sold homemade pies and loaves of bread. The aroma was heavenly, and it was so fun watching the ladies pulling baked goods out of a wood oven.

After we had been there a while, I asked if I could use the restroom. A sweet young Amish woman pointed me toward a door that led to a short hallway with another door at the end. I thanked her and made my way there.

Then I just stood there and looked at the bench where folks did their business. I stayed in there long enough to pretend I was utilizing the facility. But I just couldn't do it. Maybe it was the fact that there were paper towels instead of toilet paper. But I think mostly my resistance was due to the two makeshift holes roughly cut into the bench. I honestly thought I might get splinters if I sat down.

After I'd spent what I considered a sufficient amount of time in the tiny room, I exited. A young Amish woman was waiting for me and directed me to a sink. She pumped warm water for me to wash my hands, and she had a warm towel folded over her arm for drying my hands.

I thanked her. I bought lots of goodies that day. Then we scurried to go find another bathroom. Did I mention we were out in the middle of nowhere?

See pictures on next few pages.

Mixing business with pleasure. Beth and her grandson in Montgomery, Indiana.

The Big Spill

The name Allen Arnold is well known in the world of Christian publishing. He started the fiction program for Thomas Nelson Publishers, now a division of HarperCollins Christian Publishing. Even though he has gone on to pursue other endeavors, he is still actively involved with Christian publishing and ministry. He's even written a book — *The Story of With.* Check it out. Wise words written by a wise man.

I can't remember what year it was, but I was early into my career when 'the big spill' occurred. Allen was my publisher and boss. He was larger than life, but despite his charm and easy-going ways, he made me nervous as a cat whose tail was loitering under a rocking chair.

I do remember where 'the big spill' happened — following a conference in Indianapolis, Indiana. I don't remember which hotel, but it doesn't matter. As many times as I've reenacted one of the most embarrassing moments in my life, I would recognize the lobby bar right away.

The mishap occurred following the big awards ceremony for the coveted Carol Awards, presented by ACFW (American Christian Fiction Writers). I don't remember if I was a finalist, winner, or neither that year. Time has left me with only one recollection of that event.

Allen and I were talking about my career, and there was even mention of a new contract coming soon. It seemed a margarita was in order. My agent (at the time) handed me a tall glass. In my defense, it was too tall to house a margarita overfilled with ice. But I set the glass on the small cocktail table. I didn't sit down when Allen did. I was too busy talking with my hands and rambling on about what I wanted to write. We were still dressed in our fancy party clothes. Worth a mention since his clothes wouldn't be party worthy for long.

I hadn't even taken one sip of that drink when my hand met with the full glass, toppling it onto his side of the table, with the entire greenish-colored beverage landing in Mr. Arnold's lap.

His jaw dropped (aside from the shock, I'm sure it was plenty cold). Everyone around us gasped. I wanted the floor to crack open and swallow me up. My agent simply said, "I'll get you another drink."

When the floor didn't swallow me up, I apologized profusely as bystanders found napkins to offer the ever-gracious Allen Arnold, who insisted he was fine. He looked like he had wet his pants, so I know he was just being kind.

After returning home, having left a portion of my dignity in Indianapolis, I decided to send Allen a gift, an apology of sorts. I knew he was a big fan of hot sauce, so I chose a lovely gift set that included hot sauce and snacks. I enclosed this note: *Here is a little something hot to make up for the cold I dumped in your lap.*

His response? He thanked me for the gift and said, *"But I will never let you live this down."* And he hasn't. The story has been told many times. I've heard it from people I'd never met before. To be fair, I've told the story lots of times too.

When I dined with Allen in a group not long after the event, before I ordered a drink (of water, again in too tall of a glass with an excessive amount of ice), I passed a package to him. He was seated at the opposite end of the table from me — a seat he surely chose on purpose. My gift to him was one of those orange rain ponchos you might take on a camping trip. He didn't put it on. Guess he felt safe so far away from me.

The photo on the next page is of Allen and me years later. Gotta love him.

He still makes me nervous. I think I only make him nervous if there are tall drinks nearby.

Beth and Allen Arnold

Do the Plain People Read Amish Books?

This is a question I've posed to several Amish women. "Do you read Amish books?" While some of the ladies have confessed that they don't understand the special interest we have in their lifestyle, they did admit to reading Amish-themed novels. I've been told this type of reading is not disallowed, but that most bishops don't encourage it. But, as long as the chosen Amish books (and other genres) are clean and wholesome, no one makes a fuss.

Several mothers told me they screen all the books their preteen and teenage daughters read. Every time I have given one of my novels or a novella collection to anyone Amish, they've been thrilled. And most of the time I leave with a gift after my visits with these lovely people. I've been given cookbooks and yummy baked goods, just to name a couple of items.

The Amish also utilize libraries, and on a recent trip to Montgomery, Indiana, I ran across the tiniest library ever. There was even a copy of my very first book, *Plain Perfect.*

This is the entire library. That little cutie is my grandson. The puppy just just wandered in.

Plain Perfect!

Even the Men Read

The photo on the next page was taken with this man's permission. Although, to respect his privacy I have blurred his face.

He isn't reading one of my Amish books. Instead, he is reading one of my Texas contemporary novels, *Need You Now.*

The Gray Areas

Most people — especially readers of Amish fiction — know quite a bit about the Old Order Amish. They don't use electricity, although some utilize propane and solar panels. Phones — home and/or cell — are forbidden in some communities, but allowed for business purposes in most districts. Smart phones (with Internet, etc.) aren't allowed within any Amish communities I've visited. Teenagers are allowed a running around period (*rumpschpringe*) when they turn sixteen years old. It's a time for them to bend the rules and decide for sure if they want to be baptized into the Amish faith. And all but about five percent choose baptism.

We are familiar with the Amish dress code, which also varies from district to district. The women wear prayer coverings (*kapps*), and the Plain people speak Pennsylvania Dutch as their first language. Children (*kinner*) don't learn English until they start school when they are five years old. I could go on and on about Amish customs, traditions, and their rules (*Ordnung*), but what about the gray areas? Here are a few gray areas I have stumbled upon:

- I once asked an Amish woman how an Amish owned restaurant could get by with using electricity at their place of business, but not at home. She explained that the restaurant was co-owned by a non-Amish partner, making it acceptable to have electricity. Gray area.
- A lovely Amish woman invited me to her home. Her family had moved from a farm and into a house in town. There were other Amish nearby, co-mingling with the non-Amish (*English,* as they are referred to). Two of her sons are in that five-percent of adolescents who chose not to be baptized into the faith. As such, they can

remain close with their family. In the case of this family, the sons remained in the house with their parents. A shunning only occurs when a baptized member of a community breaks the rules. As I visited with Sarah, there wasn't any electricity, and she showed me her wringer washing machine. When it came time for me to fly back to Texas, she loaded me up with yummy snacks to take on the plane. I was still early into my Amish research at this time. I asked her if it would be all right if I wrote to her, maybe with follow-up questions. She leaned close and whispered, "You can just email me." Of course, I asked her how that was possible. She said that since her sons chose not to be baptized, they had electricity on the other side of the house, which included a computer and email. LOL. *Gray area.*

- Most people know that the Amish do not like their pictures taken, for religious reasons, and I'm sure it's annoying to have tourists in your face all the time. But I've had my picture taken with an Amish woman who had no problem posing for the photo.

So, as with any of us, rules are sometimes interpreted differently, or the person has chosen to bend the rules. But, the majority of Amish folks I've met do not want their picture taken.

When Characters Become Real

While I was writing my first series — The Daughters of the Promise — I was fortunate to make friends with a woman in Lancaster County, Pennsylvania. At first, Barbie helped me via phone calls and email. She would read my manuscripts and make corrections, which was particularly helpful because she came from an Amish upbringing. Her parents had been Old Order, then converted to Beachy Amish (less conservative Order), and that is how Barbie grew up. She later joined a non-denominational Christian church. Over time, we became good friends, and I was able to visit her several times in Paradise, a town in Lancaster County. At the time, Barbie and her husband owned a bed and breakfast, which is where I stayed during my visits. Barbie was instrumental in putting me in touch with some lovely Amish folks who spent time with me and educated me about their way of life.

I have used the names of friends in my books before. It's always fun for them to be reading along and see their name used for a character. I didn't think too much about it when I included Barbie's name in several of the Daughters of the Promise books. I also used the name of the bed and breakfast that Barbie and her husband were running at the time. Barbie's role in the stories was that she was a driver for the Amish. As others had said, she thought it was fun to be mentioned in the books.

Then it went from fun to hilarious when the lines between fiction and truth began to blur. Folks started showing up at her B&B and thought she actually drove the Amish around from place to place. Barbie had plenty of Amish friends, but she wasn't a driver for hire as portrayed in my books. I'd just used the name of her bed and breakfast, along with her name, for fun. I thought it might boost her business, even though her B&B didn't need any help from me. It was a lovely and popular place. But she got a kick out of the fact that readers assumed she was, in fact, the person in the books, right down to her occupation as hired driver.

Choosing a name can be a long process, at least for me. And sometimes character names change several times throughout the writing process until I land on one that fits. In Barbie's case, it was fun and we had some good laughs about it. But, other times, I've chosen names strictly because the name seemed to suit the character, with no other relevancy.

But it's hard to choose a name

that isn't somehow associated with someone in your life, even it was unintentional. Here are a few comments (paraphrased from memory) when I've used someone's first name.

— Hey, I would never act like that.

— Why did you make me a bad guy?

— I'm alive, not dead!

— Why did you kill me off?

— You killed my bird! (from long time BFF Renee' when I named a parrot after her parrot — Elvis. The bird died in the story, but was given an elaborate funeral complete with a fancy coffin and formal burial.

— That's not the color of my hair.

Most of the time, I never had that

person in mind when I wrote the story. It was just a good name for my character. Having said that, if I'm writing about a bad guy (or gal), I try to reach as far away as I can from anyone I know, lol.

However, I never received any complaints from Chloe, my Labrador, or other pets I've included in my books.

The Accident

Early in my career, I tried to find out as much as I could about the Plain people. I researched, made friends in Amish Country, and was blessed by the way God blew open doors of opportunity to help me get started.

One of the first things I did during a trip to Lancaster County was to pay for a ride in an Amish buggy — the type of buggy that was built more as a tour-bus buggy than what an authentic Amish ride would actually be like. And the driver may or may not have been Amish, even though he donned the traditional Amish clothing, hat, and beard.

As I got to know some Amish families and began getting invited into their homes, I mentioned that I'd never been on a 'real' buggy ride. A kind Amish woman, whom I'd gotten to know fairly well, offered to take me on a ride. It was nearing dark, but I was thrilled and didn't want to miss out on an opportunity, especially since my private tour would take me through one of the popular covered bridges.

Our journey also took us along Lincoln Highway, a busy road that runs right through the heart of

Paradise — a popular town in Lancaster County. And, sure enough, darkness fell, and my heart rate soared as cars whizzed by us. My Amish friend (we'll call her Mary) kept the horse in a steady trot and didn't seem the least bit phased by the busy highway at nighttime. I reminded myself that she travels this way all the time.

A few things ran through my mind. I'd already been told that many of the horses the Amish use to pull the buggies are retired racehorses — and when they hear a fire alarm, the animals relate the loud noise as the 'start' of a race and often take off at top speed pulling the buggy.

As we drove near the fire station,

my chest tightened, and I prayed there wouldn't be any fires that evening. Just the same, my stomach clenched most of the ride. I think I would have enjoyed the trip a lot more if it had been daylight and if the last leg of the journey hadn't been alongside a busy highway.

I breathed a sigh of relief when we pulled onto Mary's road. After she slowed the buggy to a stop, the conversation went something like this:

"Wow, that was so different than the buggy rides offered to tourists." Actually, it was a lot more bumpy than I would have predicted. "Thank you so much."

"*Ya, ya.* You're very welcome." Mary shook her head. "I'm just glad everything went okay."

Huh? Why wouldn't it have? Maybe she wasn't used to driving at night after all. I just smiled. We were safe. My stomach was beginning to settle down, and my pulse was returning to normal. I thanked her again.

She nodded, then smiled at me. "I feel *gut* about that little ride. It's the first time I've been back in the buggy since the accident."

I sat taller, swallowing hard. "The accident?"

"*Ya.*" She looked at me, then chuckled. "I've rigged a horse to a buggy hundreds of times, but a neighbor was chatting with me, and I guess I got distracted."

I don't remember the exact lingo

she used, but basically she said that she didn't have the horse and buggy hooked up properly when she got in the seat and prepared to give the horse a gentle flick of the reins. But the reins, the horse, the buggy — it wasn't set up correctly, in a way that the horse could do whatever he wanted without her having any control with the reins.

"He just took off." Mary made a sweep of her hand as she shook her head again. "I just had to hold on and hope for the best."

My jaw dropped. I was quite sure that if I'd heard this story prior to my authentic buggy ride, I would have opted out.

Mary sighed. "Eventually, I was thrown from the buggy. I got pretty banged up too." She listed her injuries, and while I was sympathetic to the pain and suffering she must have gone through, I was also thanking God repeatedly that we had arrived back at Mary's house in one piece. I exited the buggy pretty quickly.

There were other buggy rides for me, but none of them were at night or near a busy highway.

A Special Cover Shoot

Most of the covers for my books have included a cover shoot with a professional model. Sometimes, a brilliant designer at the publishing house builds the cover utilizing software for that purpose.

For my book — *His Love Endures Forever* (Book 2 in the Land of Canaan series) — the cover was being shot in Colorado because the book's setting is Colorado. My husband and I have good friends in Colorado and were excited to spend some time with them. But I had also made a suggestion to my publishing team that I was very excited about.

I realize how blessed I am to have had my BFF for over forty years. Renee' Bissmeyer carries in her memories the diary of my life. She is my soul mate, best friend, and the one person who would 'bury the body', lol. During the planning stages of the cover for *His Love Endures Forever,* Renee's daughter had recently been signed with a major modeling agency. Since my publisher hired models through an agency, I asked if they would consider Renee's daughter — Christie — as the cover model. After seeing pictures of Christie, who is gorgeous inside and out, they agreed to have her on the cover.

My husband and I flew to Colorado, and after visiting with our friends, we picked Christie up at the Denver airport a few days later. Our friend Sherry was also able to attend. Wow. It was a special day. I'd never been to a cover shoot. They take a ton of pictures with varying poses and outfits (Amish, in this case). But be still my heart. The thought of having my best friend's daughter on the cover of a book, a beautiful woman whom I'd known since she was born . . . There are no words. It was a very special occasion for me, Renee', and Christie. And I loved that my husband was able to be there, along with our friend, Sherry.

And the cover of *His Love Endures Forever* is one of my favorites, for the lovely design and fabulous photography. But also for the beauty I know is in Christie's heart. Love you, Christie, and thank you.

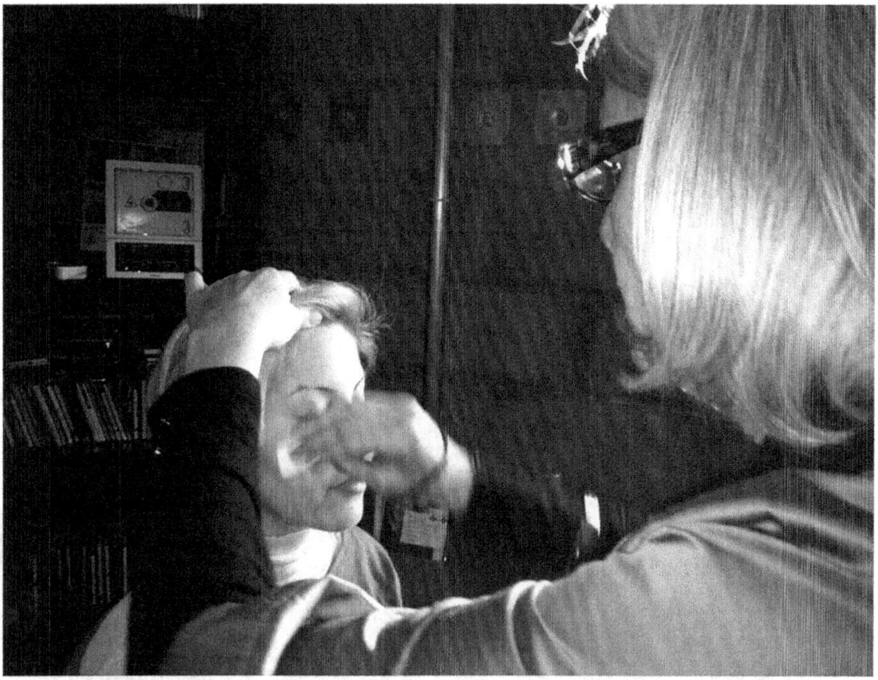

Beautiful Christie!

The End Result

And Along Came Janet

I was about a year into my publishing journey — roughly ten years ago — when I realized I needed help. Even though I had left my job as a newspaper reporter and was writing full-time from home, I couldn't keep up. In addition to writing, revising, and proofing my novels, there were a ton of backend responsibilities that needed handling. Social media was on the rise, specifically Facebook, and the promotional aspect of writing began to weigh me down.

And, it wasn't just online responsibilities that bogged me down. I needed someone to keep me on task, help me schedule events, assist at book signings, and a host of other things related to writing for a living. So I ran an ad in our local newspaper. I offered an hourly rate mostly targeted toward a high school student, and I only needed someone part-time.

I interviewed several applicants. One young lady might have worked, but there was going to be considerable training involved, and this high school student would be off to college the following year. Another sweet girl met me at McDonalds with her toddler, which

I'd told her was fine. But, it was easy to see that she had her hands full already, and I worried if she could fully commit. I wouldn't have been able to when my children were young, so I'm not placing any fault on her situation. There were others, but no one seemed to fit.

Then along came Janet. She was different from the young people I'd spoken with. We set a date to meet for lunch. For starters, she was late. Anyone who knows me well is aware that I am a stickler for punctuality. I'd honestly written her off before she arrived. I know that sounds harsh (and I probably shouldn't admit it), but it's the truth.

Janet was a sweet retired woman,

and we had several mutual acquaintances. She was soft-spoken and didn't come across as very confident. (Boy, howdy, was I wrong on that first impression). Janet didn't know much about social media platforms other than Facebook, had never set up or maintained a website (which was an attribute I had been looking for in a student assistant), and she didn't know a thing about the book industry, although she was a lovely person. But the old cliché that God works in mysterious ways was definitely in play the day I met Janet Murphy.

That evening, I told my husband that I'd struck out again. I just wasn't finding the person I had pictured in my mind. I felt a bit defeated. Then I received an email from Janet. She basically listed all the reasons that I didn't need a student assistant. She had valid points to consider. Then she listed all the reasons that I should hire her. That meek, quiet, soft-spoken person I'd met earlier wasn't who leapt from the pages of the email. This woman was confident, clearly educated (I have horrible grammar), and she went as far as to say that she would make herself irreplaceable as my assistant. THEN . . . wait for it . . .

Janet closed her email by saying that she was the person I needed to choose for the position, but she was not going to do it for what I was offering as an hourly wage. Then she presented the dollar amount she was willing to work for.

I actually laughed out loud, then read the email to my husband (what I wouldn't do to still have that email). Our conversation went something like this:

HUBBY — "Wow."

ME — "I know. Can you believe that?"

HUBBY — "She's bold. You gotta give her that."

ME — I got very quiet. Something niggled me in a way I didn't quite recognize. I know now that it was God, but at the time, I just had a gut feeling about this woman. I turned to my husband and smiled. "I'm going to hire her," I told him.

And I did.

Ten years later, Janet is everywhere, behind the scenes handling all the things that wouldn't get handled if she weren't onboard. Assistant isn't an accurate word to describe Janet. She's a marketing guru, continually educates herself in an ever-changing industry, and she coordinates promotions with my street team, Wiseman's Warriors. Janet reminds me about events, dates to remember (even birthdays), deadlines I'd surely miss otherwise, and generally keeps me on task.

Mostly, Janet is my voice of reason. I'm an idea person, and occasionally I have some good ones. But, more often than not, I get hyped up about something I have no business doing. Here's an example:

ME — "Hey, Janet, I think I'm going to open a bookstore on the square in town. Some retail space became available."

JANET — (insert heavy sigh). "No. You're not." Then she listed all the reasons why this was a bad idea. The largest of those being lack of time. And she was right all across the board.

So, in closing, I'll say this: Janet is, indeed (without a doubt), irreplaceable to me, and she wears many writing-related hats. She's everything an author needs in an assistant — again, not a good word to describe this amazing woman.

But, back to how God works in mysterious ways. How could I have ever known that Janet would become so much more than someone who works for me? God planted the seed for friendship that day we met, and it has continued to blossom over the past decade. Janet's soft-spoken nature calms my often wild and out of control creative mind. That same disposition carries over into my personal life. She has a calming effect on me when there are challenges unrelated to business. But, I would be lax if I didn't mention that Janet is also one of the funniest people I know. Her dry sense of humor has had me crying from laughter on many occasions. We've made memories we'll carry for a lifetime. I would be remiss if I didn't include this snippet in this book.

Yep. God knew what He was doing that day Janet arrived late at the restaurant. But as is His way, I couldn't foresee into the future. He knew what was best for me, and He gifted me with a person who would help me organize my life in a way that I could continue to write stories that glorify Him. But He also blessed me with a dear friend for life.

So, Janet . . . here's to another decade or two . . . maybe more, God willing.

Beth and Janet

The Ups — and the "Downs"

I'm tall. Depending on which doctor's assistant measures my height, I'm somewhere between 5'8″ and 5'10″. It seems to me they should be able to pin that down, but that's a discussion for another time. However, I enjoyed (past tense, explanation further down) wearing heels, and I have a love relationship with shoes.

On a trip to New York City, I wanted to dress the part, so I wore a modest, if not a bit shorter than usual, dress. Of course, I matched my outfit with a lovely pair of wedge heels. Not stilettos, just nice and safe four-inch wedges, which propelled me to over six-feet tall by all varying calculations. I was traveling alone from Texas and meeting my agent (at the time) at the Waldorf Astoria Hotel. I was excited to be in New York City, and as I hurriedly retrieved my carry-on bag, then made my way down the Jetway, I fell off those nice and safe wedges I'd chosen.

It happened fast. I couldn't tell you if my foot gave out, my ankle twisted, if I tripped, or if someone pushed me. (I don't think anyone pushed me. I'm just throwing that into the story as a remote possibility to make me seem less clumsy).

However it happened, I was face down in a less than flattering way with a herd of people behind me. Did I mention that shorter than usual dress? I still cringe at the visual.

Just to note — when a tall person goes down, wearing four-inch heels (even if they are wedges), getting up is no easy task. It took two big, strong men to get me to my feet. I quickly thanked them, left my wounded ego behind, and carried on. I ignored the blood running down my leg until I'd snagged a taxi. Getting a cab in NYC is also a tale for another time.

The taxi driver obliged my request for a napkin after almost having forty-two wrecks while he weaved through traffic, opening every compartment in the cab to find something for my busted knee. He finally handed me a used brown napkin that looked like it came from a used McDonald's Happy Meal. It was hard to differentiate what was blood and what was ketchup.

But, finally, I was at the Waldorf. I exited the cab and forgot about my knee. I took in the lavish hotel and my surroundings in Manhattan. I felt like *'That Girl'.* For younger readers, *That Girl* was a 1960s sitcom about an actress who moves to New York City to make it big. I was there to attend an awards gala. One of my books was a finalist for the prestigious Audie Award.

The Audio Publishers Association honors the best books in audio publishing by hosting an award ceremony. This honor is mostly for the narrators of the audiobooks, delegated by category. But there are also some authors sprinkled throughout the crowd, and a nomination gives the book exposure. Twice I've been an invited guest in New York City, where the gala was being held the two times one of my books was a finalist for the prestigious award.

I hadn't even made it up two steps to the hotel when a nice older man had me by the elbow. How lovely, I thought. I'm being escorted by one of the staff into the hotel. Once inside, he rushed me along and guided me to a sitting area, nearly out of sight, I might add. After I sat down, I saw blood trailing down my leg and pooling atop my lovely wedged shoe. The nice man, in uniform, pressed a starched white handkerchief — nothing like the napkin from the cab driver — against my bloody knee. I'd honestly forgotten about it at this point.

The doorman left me but quickly returned with bandages and ointment, then he doctored my knee. Apparently, the Waldorf doesn't care for patrons entering the building trailing blood along the way. Understandable.

I was unaffected, slouched back

into the chair, and asked the man if I could take a picture of him tending to my knee. He smiled and said it would be okay. I thanked him, while trying to be mindful of my shorter-than-usual dress, and snapped several pictures.

Oh, how I wish I had one of those photos to share with you. But, alas, I have no idea where they are since that was nearly a decade ago. But the visual will remain with me forever.

I've given up wearing my heels, even the ones that look deceivingly safe. I quit *wearing* them, but I still have them. They are on display in my closet. Who knows, perhaps I'll dust off a pair for a special occasion. And someday, I'll award them to a person who will appreciate them.

Someday.

The Red Suitcase

Only a handful of people know there is a red suitcase mentioned in every Beth Wiseman book. In the beginning, the publisher and I tried to keep it a secret, thinking we would offer a prize to anyone who could guess what tangible item was in all of my books. But, it's been over a decade, and we haven't done that. So, I think it's okay to go public and explain how the red suitcase came to be.

It was a casual conversation

among girlfriends, and I honestly can't remember enough about our discussion to even paraphrase it well. But, it was decided on our porch on a sunny afternoon that each book would have a red suitcase. My editors have all known not to edit that detail out of any books, and they usually put a smiley face next to it while revising the manuscript. My current editor usually writes, "There it is!"

I am 99% sure I haven't missed an inclusion in all of my stories. But, here's a challenge for you! If you find any book I've written — Amish or otherwise — that doesn't have a red suitcase, email me, and I'll send you a signed copy of any book you choose (that I have in stock, lol).

Happy Reading!

In my mind, this is the type of red suitcase I see.

It's Not All Glitz and Glamour

Back in the day, long before I published my first book, there were lavish book release parties. Authors were ushered around and introduced conceptually like movie stars, high profile figures who had created a work of art that catapulted them to near-stardom. At least that's what I've heard.

While I'm sure some authors enjoy that type of glitz and glamour, I assure you, most of us do not.

We have a marketing team and a publicist who work hard to get our books prime placement in retail outlets, secure blogging opportunities, arrange Facebook chats, set up radio interviews and speaking engagements, and a host of other team-related efforts. But there is no party, no champagne, no need to buy a brand new cocktail dress.

Authors are expected to work hard promoting our books via our social media platforms, networking with industry professionals, nurturing our treasured readership, and being mindful that these efforts are necessary to ensure the book gets off to a good start.

But, even though we don't get a fancy release party, there are times when we do get to enjoy a bit of that glitz and glamour.

American Christian Fiction Writers (ACFW) holds an annual conference to honor novels in relevant categories. On the evening of the awards banquet, authors, agents, publishers, guests, and the media gather for a wonderful meal and the winners of the Carol Awards are revealed. Things get a little fancy for the event. I've been fortunate to be a finalist several times, and twice I've won the coveted award. There is also an award for Agent of the Year. On the following page is a photo when both my agent and I scored a win in the same year. I won the Carol Award, and Natasha Kern won Agent of the Year.

Another lavish gathering is when the Audie Awards are presented. That trip to NYC was one of the few times I shook the dust from a pair of high heels.

Beth and her agent, Natasha Kern, at ACFW Awards Ceremony

Beth and her sister-in-law, Melody, at the Waldorf Astoria New York

Odd Places to Have Book Signings

When we think of book signing locations, libraries and bookstores come to mind. But when my first series — Daughters of the Promise — released, I wanted to think outside of the box. I live in a small town with few opportunities nearby to market my books, so I had to find places where people gathered when it wasn't convenient for me to travel far from home.

It's amazing the places people will buy books! A liquor store, for example. Now, keep in mind, this is a family-owned and operated place in a small town. It wasn't like I was selling Christian books at a big chain. I know the owners, and they are wonderful people. When they asked if I wanted to do a book signing at their place, I decided I better get permission from my publisher, lol. They gave me a thumb's up once I explained about the venue.

I noticed right away that it seemed to be mostly men coming into the store on their way home from work. Mostly, they were toting a six-pack of beer. Hmm . . . these were not the type of people who typically read my books, so I needed an angle, a marketing tool. And once I landed on the right phrase, it worked every single time.

"Hi, how are you? Would you like to buy a signed copy of my book to take home to your wife?" Then I'd eye the six-pack ever so slightly and smile.

Every one of those men bought a book, and somewhere there is a picture floating around of a man holding his beer while I sign his wife's book. Over the years, the photo has gone missing. But the memory remains.

I probably sold the most books ever at a car dealership. That could be because my husband worked there and the owners talked it up. Whatever the reason, people came! And they bought books. Some folks even browsed cars. It was a fun event, and I'm thankful to Tommy and Karen Brasher for hosting me at their dealership.

My publisher at the time talked enthusiastically about the places I found to sell books. He would tell other authors to be creative about venues, like Beth Wiseman.

Ha! I was just a small town girl trying to sell books anywhere I could. Still am.

We Don't Smoke

After my editor learned about a trend in Colorado, we decided I should write about the Amish who were migrating to the San Luis Valley. According to various sources, the Plain people were moving from Pennsylvania, Iowa, Ohio, Indiana, New York, and other states, purchasing available land that was less expensive. Particularly in Pennsylvania, the Amish were also running out of property with each new generation.

Since we have good friends in Colorado that we visit as often as we can, my husband and I decided to combine a little work and play. We traveled to Baily, Colorado to spend time with Tim and Sherry, then made plans to travel to the San Luis Valley.

Most readers familiar with the Amish genre know that things differ from state to state, and even from district to district within a state. This was most apparent when we visited two Amish families in the San Luis Valley. The first family lived in a rural area and had a dozen or so children. I'm not sure I've ever been in an Amish home when I wasn't offered cookies so that one constant seems to be prevalent across the miles.

What felt different about this first visit in San Luis Valley is the way the children stared at us as if we were from another planet. Yes, there were cookies. Yes, the family members who were present were very hospitable. But we were an oddity among them based on the curious expressions from the kiddos. The mom showed me how to use a loom, which is a device used to weave tapestry and cloth. And I saw an animal skin drying outside. It was the first time I learned that the Amish hunt. It was a question that hadn't come up in my visits to Pennsylvania.

The family owned a small general store, and I was told that the community was new and still establishing itself. We had a lovely visit, and I was told about the challenges of growing and harvesting in that area since they didn't have very much frost-free weather each year.

I had no idea that my next visit with another family would bring forth a reprimand. Miles away, there was another community newly settled. When we drove up to their driveway, I knew we were in for a completely different experience. The house looked brand new, and for lack of a better word, appeared fancy — inside and out. Although, this woman seemed guarded as she spoke to us, Lydia graciously answered my questions.

The most important take away

from the first part of our conversation was when I asked her who set the community rules. If Amish families were arriving in the area with various adaptions of the *Ordnung* (the unwritten rules the Amish live by,) then who set the standards? I already knew that there were variations in how they dressed, the colors of the buggies, window dressings (mostly green blinds in Pennsylvania), and other distinctions that weren't universal in each community.

I was told that whoever arrived in the area first set the standard for the new district. Then the woman bristled a little as she told me that they were having problems with some of the ladies in the community conforming to the rules. Specifically, some of the women were wearing their dresses too long, and this seemed to be a serious offense.

Before she could elaborate further, her husband came into the room with a stern look on his face and asked his wife if she pointed out my mistake in a book, even cited which page I'd made the error. I had mailed Lydia a copy of my first book in my Daughters of the Promise series, hoping to make her feel more comfortable when I arrived for a visit. At least, she would know that I'd done a lot of research and tried very hard to represent the Amish as authentically as possible. Lydia was introduced to me through a friend of a friend.

My heart pounded against my chest as I apologized for anything they might have found offensive in my book, *Plain Perfect.* The woman spoke barely above a whisper when she said, "We don't smoke. No one smokes. And you have men going out in the barn and smoking cigars after Sunday worship services."

I politely explained to her that in Lancaster County, Pennsylvania, smoking was a common practice following the meal on Sundays. I'd been told this by several people living in and near Paradise, Intercourse, and Bird In Hand, all Lancaster County towns. Lydia and her husband were shocked.

It would be years later before I decided to write a series in Southern Indiana. There is a place called the Catwalk in Williams, Indiana. It's a popular dam where both Amish and non-Amish folks fish. The Amish man on the next page showed up in a photo I was taking of my husband and friends at the end of the Catwalk.

Rumschpringe Boys

Most readers of Amish fiction know that teenagers are allowed a 'running around' period (*rumschpringe*) that begins when they turn sixteen years old. This is an opportunity for the teen to spread his or her wings and experience the outside world prior to choosing baptism. While some parents don't permit their children (*kinner* in Pennsylvania Dutch) to fly far from the nest, most moms and dads look the other way and allow their children freedoms not otherwise considered acceptable.

The thought process, I've been told, is that a child must see how outsiders live in order to choose — or not choose — to be baptized into the faith. Teenagers are not forced into the Amish way of life. If they choose not to be baptized into the faith, they are not shunned by their families. Shunnings only occur if a person has been baptized and refuses to adhere to the *Ordnung* (Amish bylaws that most of the Plain people know by heart). Surprising to most is the fact that less than five percent of Amish teenagers leave their Amish roots.

During the *rumschpringe,* the young people are allowed to wear

English (the word for non-Amish folks) clothes, see movies, listen to music, and cast themselves into a world not yet discovered.

On a normal day in Lancaster County, Pennsylvania, you'll likely see lots of buggies traveling around town in the traditional manner. But during one of my trips to Paradise, a town in Lancaster County, I ran across a group of boys that were definitely enjoying their *rumschpringe.* There were five fellows, and I happened upon them in a parking lot. They were standing outside their buggy, which donned Mardi Gras beads, and loud music boomed from within the buggy. Even though they wore suspenders, their shirts weren't the standard dark colors worn by Amish men. One of the boys had on a pink shirt, and they were all smoking cigarettes. They wore the type of hats the Amish wear, but instead of black loafers or boots, they had on tennis shoes. It was a confusing mishmash of Amish/English style.

I approached the boys and explained to them that I write Amish fiction and that I was aware they were in their *rumschpringe* (a word that that has a range of spellings within various Amish communities). I boldly asked if I could take their picture. Four out of the five boys agreed to let me take a photograph. One of the teens looked terrified and stood off to the side. I remember thinking at the time that he must come from a conservative family who wouldn't appreciate his new look.

Somewhere I have that picture, which I would never post in this book or any public forum. It was mostly a slice of research for me. But the visual, which remains in my mind, is filed away in my virtual memory bank to recall upon fondly.

Four boys, dressed in bright colors, their decked out buggy in the background, cigarettes angling from their mouths, shiny new tennis shoes, and boom box music filling the space around them. I haven't seen anything like that again throughout all of my travels in Amish Country.

The Meltdown

There are various versions of this quote, along with different authors who are credited: *There's nothing to writing. All you do is sit down at a typewriter and open a vein.*

In truth, that's how it feels sometimes. But the bleeding turns to hemorrhaging when you manage to turn a large chunk of words into sentences — only to lose it all to a technical glitch, or even worse, user error.

As an author of over forty books,

I've had to do plenty of rewrites. Revisions are a necessary, if not tedious, part of the process. Many years ago, I had to rewrite over twenty-thousand words because I thought I was experienced enough to put Jesus on the scene in a book. My editor thought otherwise.

In the year this book was being published, I managed to lose five-thousand words due to 'user error'. Basically, I closed down my computer before the manuscript saved to Dropbox, a software that allows users to log in on any device. It's a handy tool that I've used for a long time. If my computer crashes, I can just go to Hubby's computer, log in to Dropbox, and my manuscript is still there.

But, I was in a hurry, shut down too quickly, then ran 'Clean My Mac' (another techy program to free up space on Mac computers). I rebooted and opened the document, only to learn that NONE of my six hours' worth of beautifully written words were anywhere to be found.

That horrifying event happened at three o'clock in the afternoon. I was still crying and searching when Hubby got home from work at seven. Then I cried and searched for another four hours and didn't get to sleep until after two in the morning.

I personally don't know of any authors who haven't had to endure this type of disaster. It amazes me that I managed to go so long without having to suffer through the experience.

The next morning, I got up and rewrote it all. Some was based on memory, but surprisingly I actually increased my word count from what it was the day before. I write by the seat of my pants, meaning I don't use an outline or plan things out. I figure that if I'm surprised by events, my readers will be too. But, while writing that first draft, I'm also getting to know my characters. It isn't until the next round of writing that I revise scenes based on what I learned while I was getting to know my characters and their motivations. So rewriting that chunk that I'd lost ended up with more depth and layers, which made for a silver lining.

Although, I could do without that type of silver lining in the future.

ACKNOWLEDGMENTS

A huge thanks to my family and friends who have supported me on this amazing journey. Your love and encouragement has sustained me many times — especially during the revision process and when I'm up against a tight deadline.

To my husband, Patrick, thank you for putting up with this crazy author. I can't imagine my life without you in it, and I love you very much. You complete me.

Janet Murphy, we've worked together for over a decade. You grew into your position and trained yourself to be my most valued resource. Even more importantly, we have also nurtured a friendship that has become very important to me. Thank you for all you do to keep me sane and organized!

A big shout out to my agent, Natasha Kern. Thank you for being supportive of all my projects and a true advocate for my career. I appreciate your honesty, kindness, and friendship.

To my heavenly Father, You have blessed me more than I could have ever imagined or predicted. Thank You for placing these stories upon my heart. I hope I will continue to write books that entertain and glorify You.

ABOUT THE AUTHOR

Bestselling and award-winning author **Beth Wiseman** has sold over two million books. She is the recipient of the coveted Holt Medallion, a two-time Carol Award winner, and she has won the Inspirational Reader's Choice Award three times. Her books have been on various bestseller lists, including the ECPA (Evangelical Christian Publishers Association) and *Publishers Weekly.*

Beth and her husband are empty

nesters enjoying country life in south central Texas. Visit her online at BethWiseman.com.

The employees of Thorndike Press hope you have enjoyed this Large Print book. All our Thorndike Large Print titles are designed for easy reading, and all our books are made to last. Other Thorndike Press Large Print books are available at your library, through selected bookstores, or directly from us.

For information about titles, please call:
(800) 223-1244

or visit our website at:
gale.com/thorndike